Let's Play
I Spy

The Letters are not in order,
Just Like a Real Game of "I Spy"

i Spy With my Little Eye
Something beginning with ...

S

IS FOR

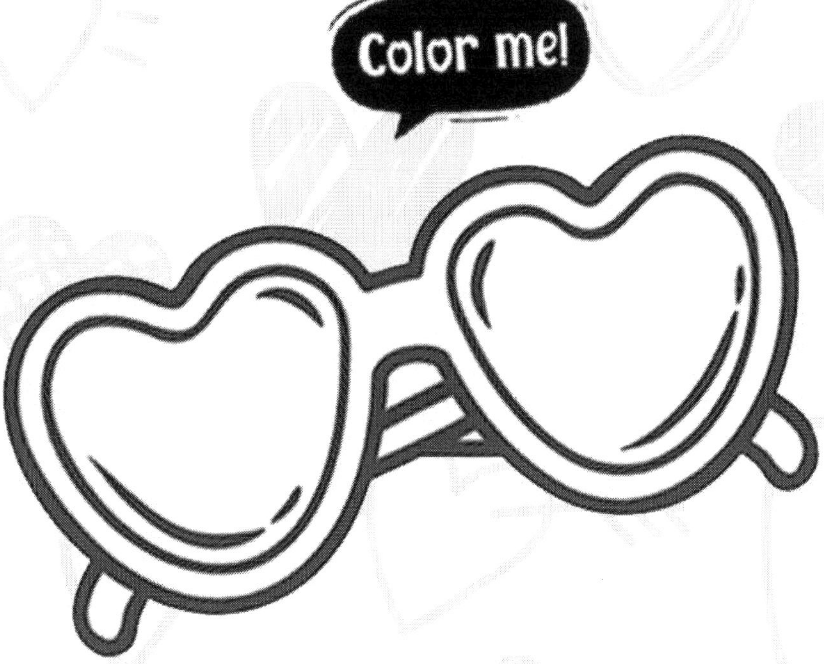

Sunglasses

i Spy With my Little Eye
Something beginning with ...

D

Color me!

D

IS FOR

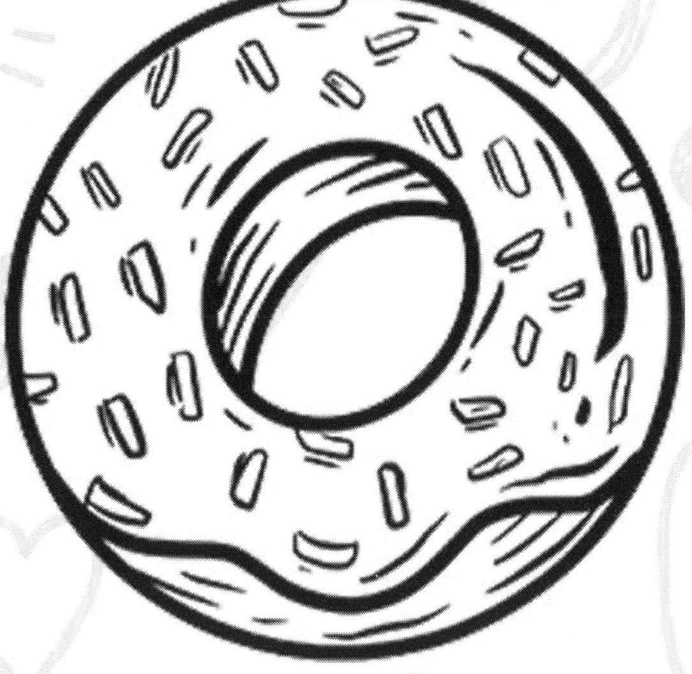

Donut

i Spy With my Little Eye
Something beginning with ...

Color me!

G

IS FOR

GiFt

i Spy With my Little Eye Something beginning with ...

B

IS FOR

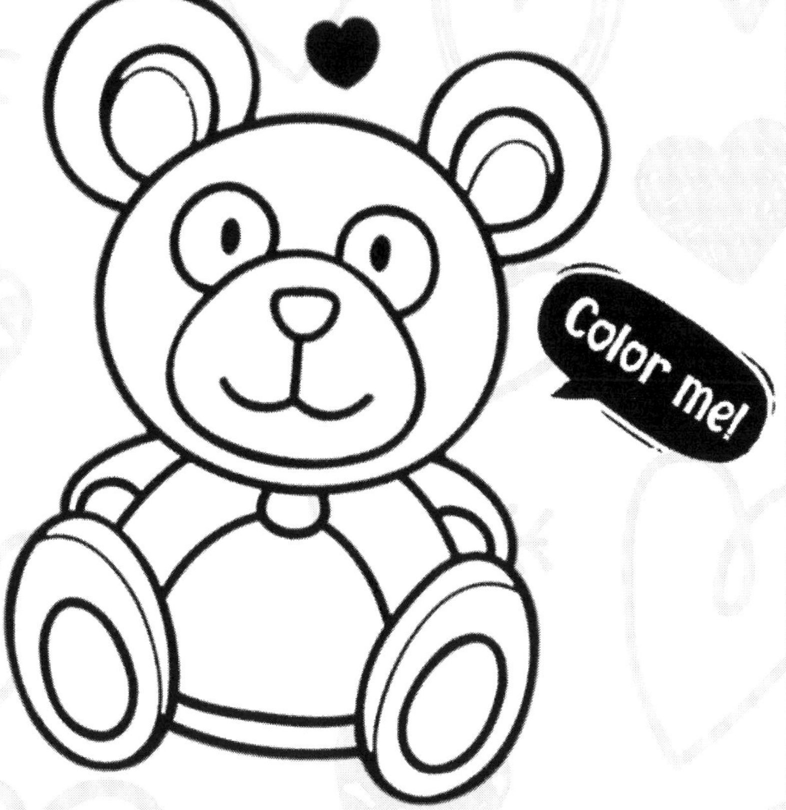

Bear

Color me!

F

IS FOR

Flamingo

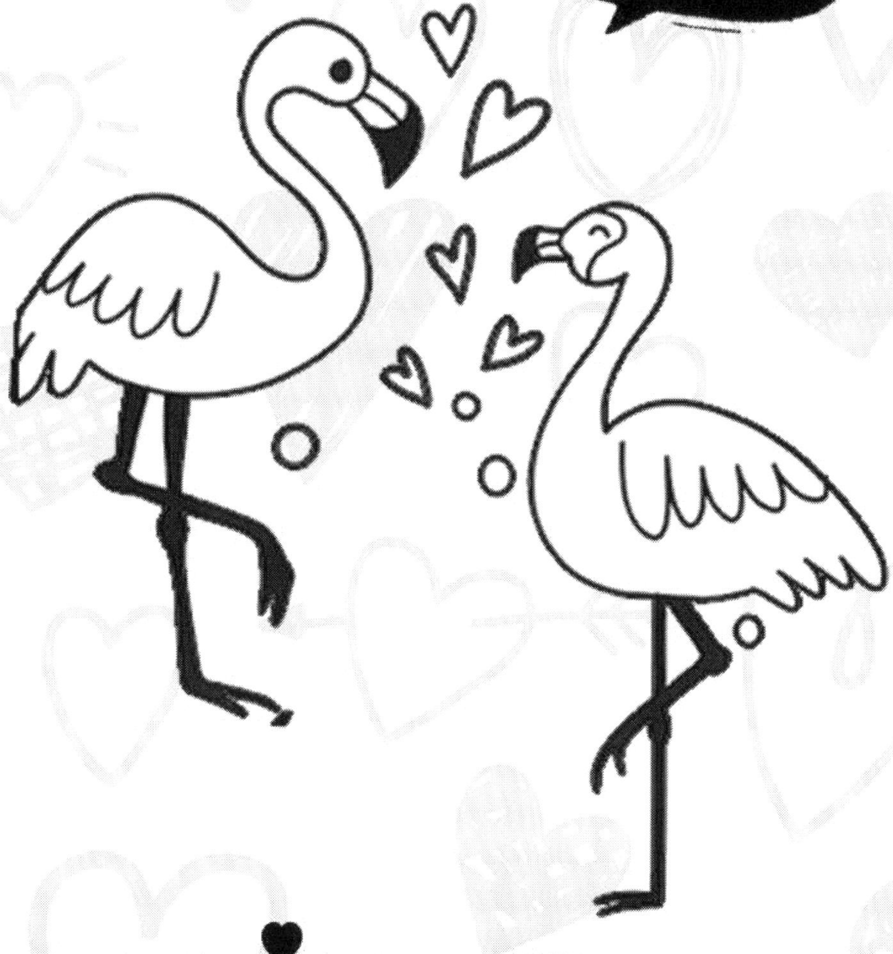

Color me!

C

IS FOR

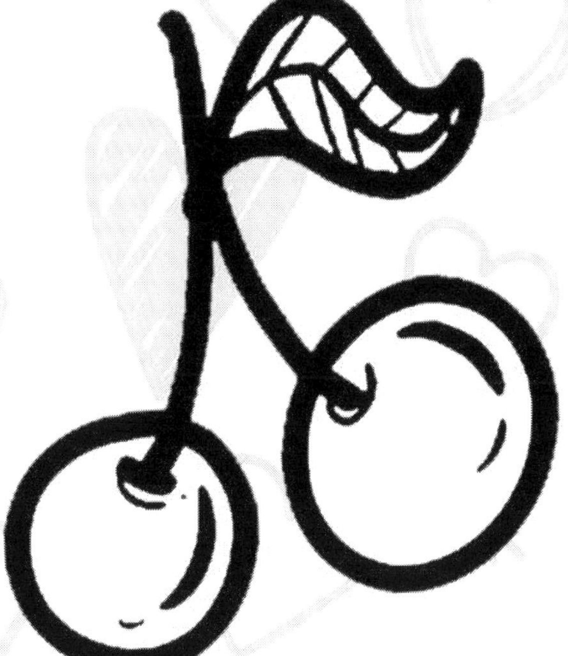

Cherry

i Spy With my Little Eye
Something beginning with ...

i Spy With my Little Eye
Something beginning with ...

Color me!

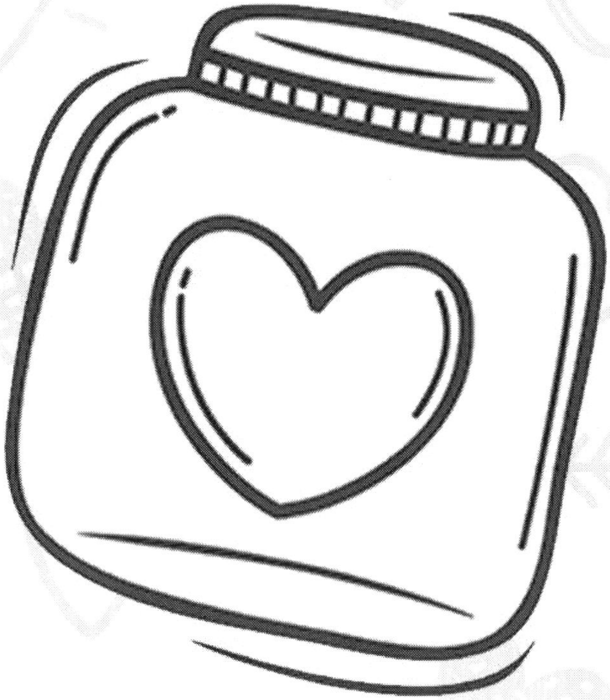

J

IS FOR

Jar

i Spy With my Little Eye Something beginning with ...

i Spy With my Little Eye Something beginning with ...

M
IS FOR

Mouse

i Spy With my Little Eye
Something beginning with ...

Color me!

N

IS FOR

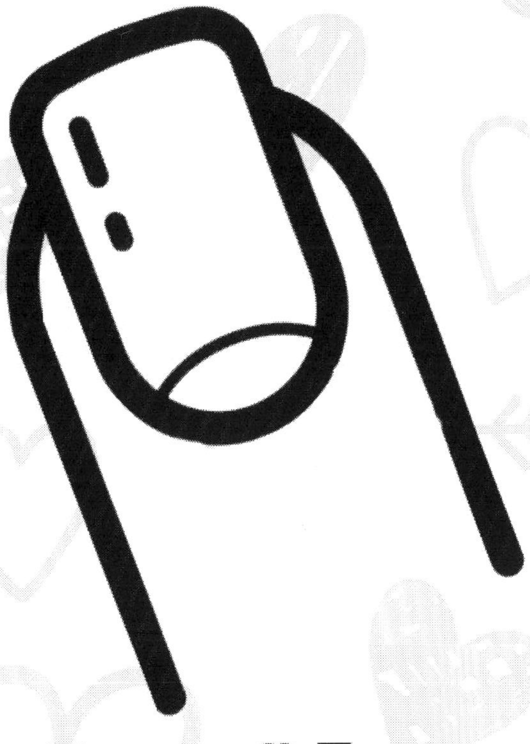

Nail

i Spy With my Little Eye
Something beginning with ...

i Spy With my Little Eye
Something beginning with ...

P

Color me!

P
IS FOR
Piano

i Spy With my Little Eye
Something beginning with ...

i Spy With my Little Eye
Something beginning with ...

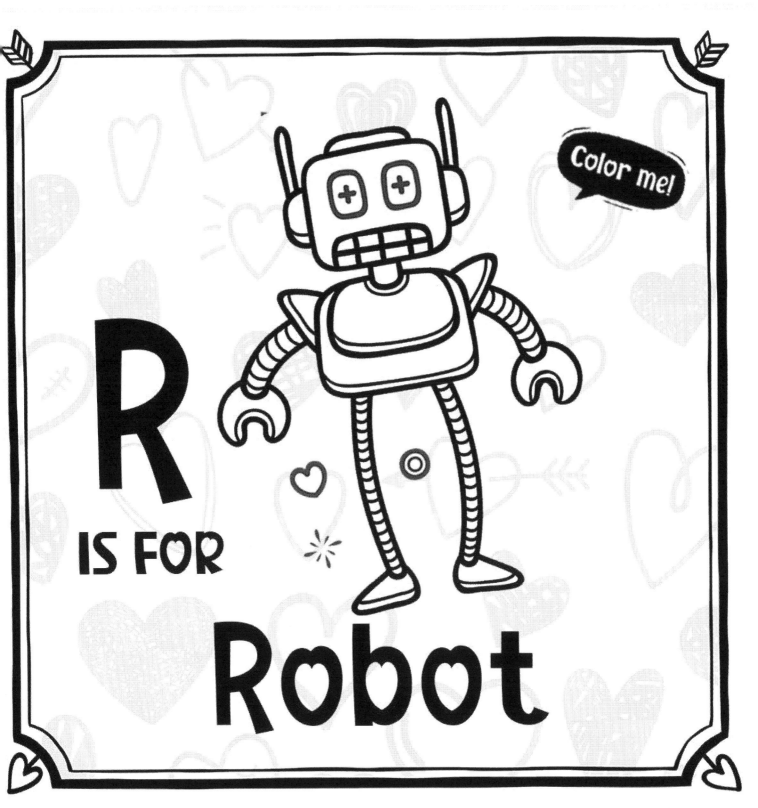

i Spy With my Little Eye Something beginning with ...

T

IS FOR

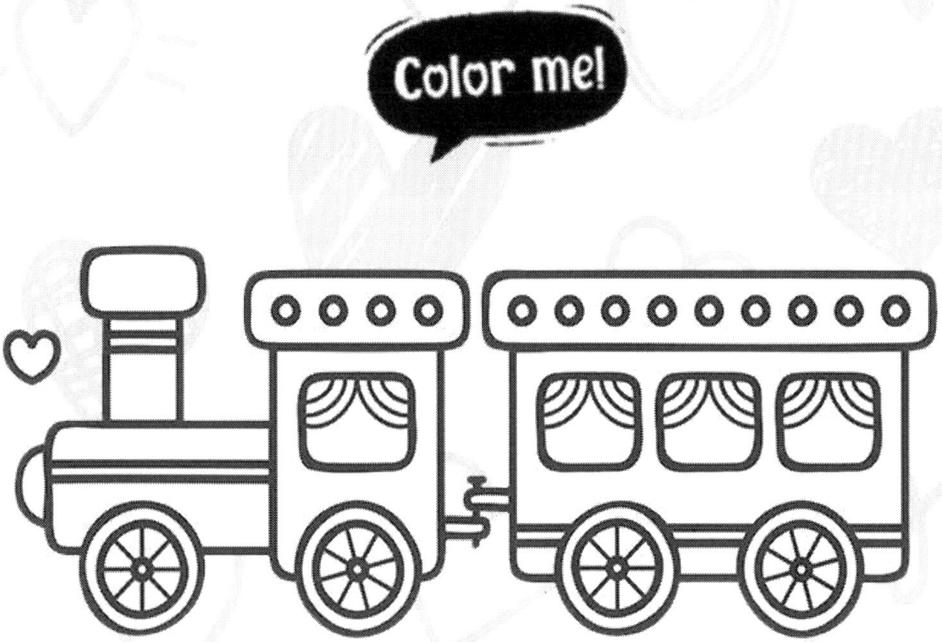

Train

i Spy With my Little Eye
Something beginning with ...

i Spy With my Little Eye
Something beginning with ...

W

i Spy With my Little Eye
Something beginning with ...

Z

IS FOR

Zebra

Color me!

i Spy With my Little Eye
Something beginning with ...

X

IS FOR

Xylophone

i Spy With my Little Eye
Something beginning with ...

i Spy With my Little Eye Something beginning with ...

Made in the USA
Middletown, DE
04 February 2022

60470470R00060